The Way Home

Richard Widerkehr

Plain View Press
P.O. 42255
Austin, TX 78704

plainviewpress.net
pk@plainviewpress.net
512-441-2452

Copyright © 2011 Richard Widerkehr. All rights reserved under International and Pan-American Copyright Conventions. No part of this book may be reproduced or distributed in any form or by any means, or stored in a data base or retrieval system, without written permission from the author. All rights, including electronic, are reserved by the author and publisher.

ISBN: 978-1-935514-70-1
Library of Congress Number: 2010936382

Cover art: *alien boy,* CB Follet
Cover design by Susan Bright

The Way Home

Richard Widerkehr

Who will bear witness for the witness?

Paul Celan

Acknowledgments:

My gratitude to these publications for printing these poems:

"Disappearances" in *Passages North*; "You," "Going," "Landings," "Breughel's Harvesters," and "Late Snow" in *The Bridge*; "Night Fields" in *Writers' Forum*; "The Hallway," "Into the Rain," "The End of the Field," "Looking for My Sister," "Where the Voices Took Her," and part one of "Afterward" in *Crab Creek Review*; "Drops on the Window" in *Jeopardy*; "Two Poems for My Father" in *Bellingham Review*; "The Way Home" in *Bitterroot*; "Into the Forest" in *Black Buzzard Review*; part two of "Afterward" in *Red Rock Review*; the poems in part four of this book in *Mountain*, a chapbook published by Pudding House Publications (2006); and "Night Fields," "Disappearances," "Coots," "Into the Forest," "Into the Rain," "Landings," and "The End of the Field" in *Disappearances*, a chapbook published by Radiolarian Press (1996, 2003).

"Disappearances" and "The Way Home" were reprinted in *Northwest Poets and Artists Calendar*; "Disappearances" was reprinted in *Northwinds Anthology*; "You" was reprinted in *Pontoon*; "Breughel's Harvesters" and "You" won awards in *The Bridge's* annual poetry contests; "Looking for My Sister," "The Way Home," "Disappearances," and "The End of the Field" were reprinted in *The Northwest Renaissance Poets*, volume X, and "Breughel's Harvesters" and "Landings" were reprinted in volume XVI. "Looking for My Sister" was reprinted in the tenth anniversary edition of *The Northwest Renaissance Poets*.

The epigraph by Paul Celan was cited by Alicia Ostriker in "Ecclesiastes as Witness: A Personal Essay" in *American Poetry Review*, January/February, 2005.

Many people helped over the years with encouragement and suggestions on these poems. I want to especially thank Linda Ford, Gayle Kaune, Patricia Hooper, and Jay Klokker. Gayle Kaune helped out with the arrangement of poems in this book. Lana Hechtman-Ayers read the manuscript and referred me to Plain View Press.

Dedicated to my mother, father, and sister,

and to Linda

Prologue

Our house believes its first life was the best.
Rain tasted like licorice, not regret.
The smell of rain, my sister twirling in the basement,
doing her pirouettes. Rain on the roof meant no less
than flimsy wind or stars that hadn't wept,
stubborn as grains of sand. The angels
of our stucco walls, the steady
thrumming of my Magnavox, storms that swept
in from the frozen river, a screen door, restive
when left ajar, the eaves that held
the amorous swallows, busy as time's best
arrows—all these ebbed
from day to night, from night to day, from windows, steps,
from seven times seven, our height measured in pencil
on the kitchen wall, which held all the stories that kept
rising, till the house couldn't rest.
It spelled out what happened, and what came next.

Contents

    Prologue   7

I

    Hansel and Gretel   13
    The Snow Twin   15
    Going   16
    Some Other Life   17
    Hostages To Fortune   18
    Drops On the Window   19
    The Hallway   20
    Sleeping Beauty Roses   22
    Looking For My Sister   24
    Afterward   25
    Where the Voices Took Her   26

II

    You   29
    Isabel   31
    Molly   33
    Safety   34
    Homeless   36
    To Deirdre In Seclusion   37
    Two   39

III

    Night Fields   43
    Disappearances   44
    Coots   45
    Into the Forest   46
    Into the Rain   47
    Landings   48

Late Snow	49
Breughel's Harvesters	50
The Way Home	51
The End Of the Field	52
Two Poems For My Father	53

IV

Snapshot	59
Doors	60
Pishke	61
"Come Here," Said the Burning Angel, and You Said, "Here I Am"	63
My Father In His Office	65
February	67
Mountain	68
Pony	70
What With the Snow	71
The Will	73
Three Wishes	75
Boxer Shorts	76
Moses Standing On His Head	77
Remember Me	79
Making Your Bed	81
Ledger	82
Black Clarinet	83
Snow	85
No Clouds, No Wind	86
La Jolla	88
A Big Fir Tree, Uprooted	89
Shadow Boxing	91
Crossing the Water	92
Six Degrees Of Freedom	93
Horses Grazing	94
Blue As Twilight	95

About the Author	97

I

Hansel and Gretel

No one mentions our first mother
or why there's a famine in the land.
No wonder I stand in doorways,
pockets filled with flints and bread crumbs.

The witch is anorexic.
All this fuss about
sugar windows, icing,
and kids good enough to eat.

Each morning I hold out
the chicken bone
she takes for my finger. Still
not fat enough.

Then, one day
the screaming starts,
and, caged behind a grate,
I can't see who it is.

I've heard Gretel cry,
but not this high, thin crackling.

*Hansel, we'll fly away
on the back of a white duck
over the wide river
with no stones.*

*One at a time. The white duck
can't carry us both.*

*We'll give Father
the witch's pearls and rubies.*

*We'll feed the birds
their crumbs and separate pebbles.*

*If we live, neither one of us
shall marry.*

The Snow Twin

For my sister

Snow falls on a street, as it happens, perfect—
dark Parkside spun by its snow twin, perfect.

When I ran out, breathing the scent of snow,
the elms of absence held themselves in, perfect.

I woke to your ward of domes and eyes,
walking its halls, your windows closed in, perfect.

A voice makes you pay for the color black.
Mostly, you're quiet—snow's decision, perfect.

Firmly, you push Mom out of her living room.
Holding the keys, you won't go back in—perfect!

You take no meds. Sometimes you live on air.
On your blank page, what stays unwritten, perfect?

A strict October day, Dad stares straight ahead—
our year of snow about to begin, perfect.

Age two and four, dressed for a family picture,
held in Mom's anxious lap, two children, perfect.

I can't even ask you about the snow—
huge flakes falling? Nothing about them perfect.

My name, it means *strength*; our last name, *return*.
In what language can our past have been perfect?

Going

It was morning when we set out, riding
under the el. In the back seat,
Chloe and I bickered over
who was on whose side. An overpass,
a railroad yard, the smell of fresh bread—
"Take the Skyway," we shouted
as the bridge came up, and we drove through
its lattice of strange shadows,
rivets big as our wrists. On one side
of the river, the red lines of the Wrigley sign
slid down like skywriting; on the other,
blue buildings smudged themselves
on the air. We were up high
as they were, our tires whining, the river
wrinkled and silky. We were going
into the city.
                        One night we came back late
and got off the bridge. My father
stopped the car by a warehouse
near the railroad yard. I had to throw up.
It was winter. Standing beside me, no coat on,
he held my shoulders as I shivered
and stared at the city, its lights floating,
the bridge rippling as if it were an airfield
and we were going there.

Some Other Life

This sun-struck girl and this boy frowning—
they aren't you and me, Chloe,
though the car seems about right,
'48 Olds, big, swept back, waiting
to haul a load of grapefruit
to the market.

This is someone else's picture,
some other life. These aren't
the carrots and tomatoes we counted
on the Ryders' farm on Cape Cod,
those summer mornings
when we were kids.

These are grapefruit—
the baskets so clean and bright,
even in black and white, the grapefruit
seem to glow. The car's
parked halfway across a road,
a gray sedan

about to head out,
the kids posed dutifully
for a picture—one last picture—
so a stranger can steal a glance
or gaze at them fondly,
fifty years later.

Hostages to Fortune

Tchik-a-tchik, his talk in fits and starts, a hypomanic lawn sprinkler,
>not quite catching up with his thoughts.

All my life, I took it. I'm not going to take it.
>*Federal hand-outs, fat-cat farmers, welfare mothers.*
African-Americans. If they're African-American, I'm Israeli-American.
>*And you, you cry about atrocities.*

You're staring at a spot on his forehead, a global positioning system,
>a mirror lasering scorn.

>*When a man has kids, he gives hostages to fortune.*

What you told him: how you went into
>the level playing fields of regret, tasting the black waters,
and how you came back, like Lazarus.

>*Your sister's a survivor. You're not.*

What you didn't say. Once, there was a boy
>whose silence was a fact like rain, the shush of cars
on wet streets, as if to speak were a threat to the government
>of stars and dark, arching elm trees on Parkside
near Seven Mile Road and Livernois.

>*She's spontaneous. You're studied.*

A black stream in a snowy field,
>erases the hidden staircase of memory,
a wrought-iron railing, a window seat of witness,
>stars that fell into the black hole
of that vast balance sheet of scars and slights,
till you became the devil's advocate for silence—
a pawn, a hostage, a well,
>a stone dropped into that well,
ripples in that well.

Drops on the Window

They shivered when they hit the window,
slid some, and stayed still
long after it stopped raining.
I twisted the string from the window shade,
twisted and let it go,
flicking the boring thing with my fingers.

I wasn't supposed to sit on the windowsill.
I knew that. I'd been spanked
once. But the window
felt cool and close. Outside,
cars hissed on the wet, black street,
and I counted Chevy Belairs, Buick Specials.
The world felt close.

Then the wind started, and the big drops
ran down the window, ticking
and bumping like thimbles,
skittery. They sped, stopped, skipped,
then opened like zippers.
The drops stayed on the side
of the window, close—
the glass under my fingers
cool as my mother's face.

The Hallway

I'm back in my old bed
in Forest Hills, New York. It's almost morning.
In the hallway, watery shadows
won't let me get up. They drift down
from the ceiling in the foyer,
the chifforobe with its four thin legs.
There's the humming
of the elevator,
                      and look, I'm up
near the ceiling, floating because
that's what shadows do
and I can do it, having had
years of practice when my parents
weren't looking—finding the right updraft,
staying under the white ceiling, always
surprised when it happens
and it's Up You Go—
                      over the rainspouts
and rooftops and smoky bridges at dawn,
gliding low, though somehow to stay up here
I've got to remember
Zuckertort's beautiful nineteen-move combination
with the queen and rook sacrifice
ending in mate, and hi there, Queensboro Bridge
with your girders and shadows, I've got to
keep going, for it seems I remember
the time Aunt Helen threw a chair
across the blonde-oak, dining-room table
we go round and round, Chloe,
though I don't know why they're fighting
and why Helen doesn't want to Go Back In
and why Mom's eyes squinch in when she says Bellevue
and why Dad's frown is like the hallway
and why I keep saying our address,
99-21 67th Road.

The elevator door
bangs open—then a sigh.
My father's sitting on my bed,
a dab of shaving cream on one ear.
He smiles, and I smile back, half-woozy,
not wanting to get up.

Sleeping Beauty Roses

Late August, the elm trees arched in the heat,
leaves fat as dinner plates—
I thought there would be more time.
I could read or while away the hours
on a poem, revise
it over and over, till it was right.

Back then it was never right,
the tone, a sound, and to get away from the heat,
I'd go down to the basement. A vise
on a tool bench, clamped on nothing; a Michigan license plate
from—when? A piano that wasn't ours
in a long dance room with a wooden floor. It was time

to come to dinner. Soon it would be time
to ask him questions, since he was always right.
And then there'd be hours
of TV—"Mysterns and Westeries," we called them. The heat
of his coffee cup I brought him, Mom handing us plates
of pie, the smell of cinnamon. I could revise

all this forever, add some violence, some sex, revise
our lives into *77 Sunset Strip*. There'd be time
for walks to Livernois and heaping plates
of stories like trips to Tomorrowland. He was right—
you always knew who the killer was. If you couldn't stand the heat,
you got out of the.... But she didn't. She was ours,

we were hers. Why didn't she leave? Hours
of cooking, cleaning—"Where did it go?" she asks. Grandma advised
her to leave, offered to take care of us kids. But the heat
of their love-hate had pulled them out of time,
made them a fact like death or Texas. She couldn't get it right.
"I should have...." But there were plates

to wash and tomorrow's good buy on fine, blue plates
from Italy. She'd gather up the hours,
like Sleeping Beauty Roses, make them come out, if not right,
well, almost. So I might write some lines, revised
by grief's oblique, dark leaves, recall the times
she took us swimming at Kensington, huge trees in the heat

by a streetlight, summer's fragile dinner plates, the heat
unbroken. There's time. What's twenty-four hours
times sixty minutes, sixty heartbeats? It's all right. Don't revise.

Looking for My Sister

My father and I hunt in the darkness
for Chloe, who sleeps in her van.
I once thought he created
this city, walking into it each morning,
hauling it back each night, so Chloe
and I could clog the drains on Grandma's terrace,
floating our toy ships. Now in the darkness,
sweat falls from my father's eyes
as we trudge by men offering to rinse
our misty eyeglasses, holding their rags out
to be kissed.
                  Here she is, lying between
two buildings, under a piece of corrugated tin
slanting from one wall to another. We stare
at her light breathing, her tightly-closed eyes.
My God, she's got her *sleepy-top*,
that tattered, old pajama top she wrapped
around the thumb. Somewhere a black wing
tears into the sky the way a flock
of dunlins turns from white to black. But here
the sky goes blue-black, black, blue-black,
and we can't see her.

Afterward

1

She's been out there all night in the snow.
The swing is her childhood swing.
When we ask if she's going to do that all night,
she says, "That's the general idea."
We go out with trays of steaming mugs
and TV dinners. She says the meat
costs twenty dollars a pound. She doesn't
eat meat. We offer quilts, books, lawn chairs,
framed certificates from forty years ago.
She goes on swinging. The snow
keeps falling. She says there's a man
in the house with a butcher's knife who last night
asked her to make her mark on his blade.
She says she told him her initials.

2

Now the snow's stopped falling,
fields and roofs and branches thickly laden—
froth blown from the fir trees
goes like an afterthought.
I can't tell if the silence
is a survivor's stubborn gaze
or mute astonishment. There was gaiety
and something else.
                        Chloe,
all day I've gone through letters
from twenty years ago, before
the voices took you. You wrote me
from Niagara Falls—an ocean
stood on end, you said,
no before or after.

Where the Voices Took Her

Where the air people
build their flowery cities; where llamas
don't have nasty habits but stare
out of their dark eyes;
where Shangri-la falls away in snowfields
and she slides down the white slopes,
and the planet's radioactive waste
can't seep through the snow;
where ghost dancers
resurrect the dreaming herds
whose white clouds block the sun;
where everyone's ears are ringing with a hum
like a TV turned down low;
where lovers get married on mountaintops,
wearing T-shirts, shorts, sunglasses,
and long, dark preacher coats—
they drink champagne and climb a sheer rock face
as the sun comes out and the hidden lakes
lie scraped of all their pain.

Someday I'll cross her frozen fields—
climbing gear dangling from my neck.
I'll squeeze the needled
sunlight in my fist and walk through
her stampeding clouds, her avalanche of sighs.
Come back, come back.

II

You

1

Ben's eyes are wide, pale, as if to him
lymph were something perfect. He doesn't tell me
about the thrilling days of yesteryear—
a medic on a helicopter,

he had to push the wounded out the doors.
In a flat voice, he mentions, "oval lift-bodies,"
his inventions. He says, "Schizophrenics
don't get letters." Faint smile.

I'm so glad he's never
shown me his apartment, or I'd have to
tell you about that, too. I listen to him

like a starless night, like mother's milk,
work that's never done. Please forgive
my words on this unblank page.

2

These days I write things down in notebooks
I don't show anyone. All the perfect words
can go to hell, where I've gone—
with Ron who hears voices saying, *Go,*

don't go, or *Asshole, asshole...* Down here
with Ben whose blue eyes turn me
to stone. Or to water. He mentions
angels with condominiums,

says, "Computers are individuals, too."
I'm paid money to feel things
for my people. To you it must

seem in bad taste to talk like this.
But though their eyes look different,
they feel things, too.

3

You, way up there in your blue-dark sky,
tonight I want to tell you how we people
feel sometimes. You with no eyes or lips—
what's the matter, star?
                         One night I walked
down a driveway. There were flowers,
an arbor... We leave places
and go out in cities, heaping stones.
You, with your different perspective,

can you feel loss or blame? To you
it must seem strange, these things called "lives."
And yet not sad? Perhaps our wish

to be called back to what we were
lives on—in streets, trees, archways—or when
someone tells you how things are.

Isabel

With your long, brown bangs,
with your face of chert,
with your hissing and shouting, "Get away! Shut up, Puta."
With your endless scrubbing the kitchen sink,
with your washing your face
in the kitchen sink.

The nurse has sent me to take you to your room—
the other patients are getting upset.
"You're making too much noise," I say.
You say you can't help it.
Righteous indignation.
Clouds form in front of the moon.

You yelled "Puta" when we sang "Happy Birthday"
to Jacob in the kitchen.
Shouting, you strewed his clean laundry
down the hall.

"I'm not going to argue with you," I say.
"I'm going to get help."

"You're going to need lots of help."
A twist of the mouth, a sneer.

When I bring the nurse, you point at me
and say: "I want you to write him up."

I write myself up, guilty as charged.
I told you to go to your room.
Tell the moon to wipe me clean of words.
Tell the sea to beat against the walls
of my head.

You who live with shouts and curses,
whom unseen Putas assail day and night,
whose shouts make you stronger,
who never seem to tire and the meds don't touch—
you who mutter, "Puta, don't mess with my bones."

Molly

When I pound the walls, you know me.
When I cut on myself, it's real.
I can't tell you how someone hurt me.
I can't tell the words how to feel.

The pain God can't believe—
if he heard me, he wouldn't come near.
The cuts on my legs make me see
what I am, what my life means.

Let me do what I have to do.
I can't tell you how someone hurt me.
The walls and the cuts know how to feel.
When I pound the walls, you know me.

Safety

I hear you, but can't see you. Just a speck.
Only my outline of your paltry lance
against the sun. And when my door gets locked,
I hide your picture, since all evidence
gets taken in the night. They call that safety.
I've had it with their sleep meds, carpet rides.
I crack the capsules open, lick the powder,
urging my tired horse to a wintry sea.
But no, that's you. I get mixed up. No wonder,
what with all their brave, new diagnoses—
Schizoaffective versus Bipolar,
Personality Disorder, Cluster B.
But to resume. Oh, Muse of Get-Me-Out-
Of-Here, fly to me now! Help me to tell
how the brave Hector fell into their clutches
and in the end rode free. How they asked him
twenty questions. "Sign here, and here." At night,
they shined their flashlights, "Q fifteen," they call it,
every fifteen minutes. They say we rode
our white mare naked on I-5. Got restrained
in the E.R. Bit a young kiddo doc.
"You shouldn't put your finger in my mouth,"
I said. They wrote down "antisocial," claimed
we waved a spike, the tip of our worn spiral
notebook. What memoir can acquit us? Enough,
enough! Ah, Hector, how they strapped us down
and jilted us with winds of cinnamon.
Inapsidryl, ten milligrams. They struck
and struck again, and still it took six pigs
to put us down. Poor Doctor Pussywhip,
licking his finger like a pup. And hope,
what hope now, Hector? Still, we know it's time
to take our meds or cheek them, get our levels,

work the program, find our mare and, spurning
the solarium, ride a white line down
the freeway to that orchard near Chelan.
Perhaps, we'll live on plums, not milk, spare tires,
pumpkin seeds, and starlings, as they fed me.

Homeless

You want a warm coat for your grief.
On Railroad Avenue, you stop me
and ask, "Don't I know you?
Didn't you once sing that song?"

No, but I wonder.
And the closet you hid in
up on the unit, scared of the voices—
was that you, also?

April, in its thin rags,
has stopped asking for spare change,
while the stars in their lonely arcs
just want to lie down in the grass.

Friend, do I know you?
Today a street. Tomorrow a star.

To Deirdre in Seclusion

My train passes through
cities and clouds,
and you're in the quiet room.

Mom tells me,
"If—when I pop off—
give Chloe a call."

Sign on your door:
"It's OK to be who you are
so long as it benefits you."

Last week you punched Joe.
We found a scissors
woven into your chair.

Dad says let her fall.
You want someone to take you
out for a cigarette.

Mustard-yellow fields.
Dad says he always
bet on himself.

"When I bet on someone else—"
He shrugs. Crosses you
painted on your door.

A siding near Aurora—
an old orchard,
gnarled, blossoming trees.

A red-tailed hawk
lit from
underneath.

Chloe's ballet classes—
"She should've
had more training," Mom says,

pushing the last piece
of Boston cream pie toward me.
"Eat that. Momma says."

Last week, Chloe hugged her—
for the first time, she asked
about Mom's medications.

Mom showed her
the printout: heart meds
and Coumadin to break up blood clots.

They talked for two hours
while Dad ate Tootsie Rolls
and waited in the motel office.

At the train station,
Mom says,
"Goodbye, traveler."

Two

There was a sister, a brother,
entering one room, then another.
There were six bridges and three rivers,
saying goodbye forever.

Entering one room, then another
(the cat clock ticked in her room,
saying goodbye forever),
he ran and she followed.

The cat clock ticking and grinning,
a day they threw leaves and he left—
when he ran, she followed
the cat's eyes back and forth.

A day they threw leaves and he left,
crossing bridges and rivers,
(the cat's eyes back and forth),
she saw a shadow no one saw.

Crossing bridges and rivers,
the East River wrinkled and silky,
she saw a shadow no one saw
on the kitchen's blue linoleum,

the East River wrinkled and silky.
It said, *Six bridges, three rivers,*
a kitchen's blue linoleum.
There was a sister, a brother.

III

Night Fields

She was riding the rope swing
under the fir tree, and somewhere a branch
was creaking. She gazed at the tree
with its gray bark, up where the branches
started, thirty feet high. A rushing
went through them. They'd been quiet
at her window, but now they were
too loud, too close, like the sea.
The goats, staked out, munched on
their weeds; and she leaned into the dark,
closing her eyes as if she knew
trees can grow tired of being trees,
knew they can toss and heave
and take her through the dark fields.

Disappearances

> *Dunlin—medium-sized sandpiper....*
> *Large flocks are found on mud-flats....*
> *If a hawk flushes them, they cluster in a tight group,*
> *twisting and swirling in the air.*
>   *Audubon Society Field Guide to North American Birds*

They were moving over the water—
a thin, dark cloud maybe a mile long,
slowly flattening out. And through
the binoculars, we saw dunlins
flung like leaves, so many
flickering and vying.
     All at once,
the cloud flipped over—white, black, white—
in the sunlight fading to nothing.
They came slanting up, a sleeve pulled inside out,
unraveling. "Special effects," you said,
though the birds didn't seem to know
they were doing anything special,
flashing in and out of this life and some
second life, over gray water.

Coots

As I walk down the road, my boots
crunch on the gravel, a good sound like knowing
I'll sleep when I'm tired. The sun
shows a little through the cloud cover.
The wet road gleams. Moss-covered branches,
the hills starting to get green—
things seem so deep inside themselves,
it's as if I'd never seen them.
Nearing the shoreline, I rouse the coots,
and they take running jumps off the dock—
fat, black-frocked chickens
riding their bicycles, flapping and clucking,
then floating off, low in the water,
as the lake becomes itself again.

Into the Forest

What if the road didn't end? What if
the woods went on and the rain kept falling?
What if we drove deeper into the forest,
gray and green dissolving in mist?
What if a curve sign with the word "Bliss"
came up, just past a ghost town called
Washington? What if the rain
on the windshield muttered, "Change your name"?
What if the pebbles flung up by our tires
said, "Lucky Seven"? What if the harp music
on the tape deck really were the sound
of defrocked angels slashing tires
in the rain? What if when we tried to speak,
ferns uncurled from under our tongues?

Into the Rain

Rain's falling steadily. It steams
on the road; it slides off the roof and drips
onto the plastic covering the woodpile.
The fir trees lift their enormous sleeves
full of sleep, and the rain goes on and on,
riding in diagonals into the lake,
coating the flat, stubby fir needles
that glisten by the window and stand on end.
The rain doesn't stop; and we lie in bed
and we don't stop going deeper into each other,
getting closer and closer, till either
the rain becomes our quiet breathing
or we're not ourselves but deep inside the rain,
unlikely dreamers who've forgotten breakfast.

Landings

Sometimes I go to the end of gray
ramshackle docks, half-buried landings,
and gaze across the frozen lake
where a few geese seem to walk on water.
Blurry in the binoculars, they drift
through the ice and mist as if
indifferent to this world and the next.
Not me; not yet. The geese
idly bend and peck with a gawky grace.
As they go, I remember
deer standing in dry leaves,
the heat of late summer, and sleep,
reasons for sleep.

Late Snow

We stood under the streetlight as snow
filled the alley, falling on the fir trees,
hissing lightly—cars and roofs
half-hidden, and so were the puffed-up
lids of garbage cans. The snow
fell fast and light, heavy and slow,
glowing on the ground and in the sky.
The tips of fir trees swung
as we stared up. Turning,
you handed me a piece of chocolate—
I picked off the foil
and bit in.

Breughel's Harvesters

The harvest's half-over; there isn't
a sound for miles. In the heat,
men and women sit under
the one tree, peaceful and completely
absorbed, almost like cattle.
It's as if they've always
been here, having once reached
for a basket or
held up a wooden spoon. One man
lies sprawled on his back, head lolled
to one side. A woman in black
stares off.
               In the fields,
women in white blouses
have stooped down beside triangular
ricks; a few men, heads down,
faces half-hidden, having leant out
with their scythes, seem unlikely
to move ever. One man
holding a jug stands in the swath
between two walls of wheat.
Beyond him is the world—
a little town, a bay, a few
faint outlines of ships.

                       The only tree
stands cool and dark, each leaf
flat and distinct, casting no shadow,
existing somewhere past labor
and grief, where the bronze crickets
can't sing and that procession
just visible beyond the wheat
isn't going away but somehow floats
up past two geese, their wings outstretched
like dark, brown sleeves.

The Way Home

Sometimes when I walk home on the road,
mist sits in the hills, dividing their dark green
from darker green. There's the lake,
then hills and mist and hills and sky—
the white mist like a river floating sideways
up the hills, spread out in billows,
thinning into bits and scraps. It's as if
things had become clearer, more themselves.
The gray sky lets in more light than I expect.
It seems so close, piled up on the hills
like a second lake. And someday I'll go
far away, not on a road, maybe deeper
into green and white, and there won't be
windows, doorsills, paper, socks, or spoons.

The End of the Field

Across the field, the fir trees
don't exactly make a wall. Thick and quiet,
the heavy branches hardly lift or bend.
If you came closer, they might draw you in
with a vague negligence, as if your being there
were final, since trees have their reasons
for being there, too. The field's
bare and quiet, no birds or squirrels about.

It doesn't make sense to say the trees wait.
They don't go on and on like a forest.
Looking at them, I try to imagine
a mood that isn't human, a thought
turned to branches, whose idea of living
is to stay at the end of the field.

Two Poems for My Father

    1   Observation Deck

Times we saw him off,
I strained to see his face.
We pumped quarters in the insurance machine
till the shiny silver printed a pink page.

We waved, then hooked our fingers
in the cyclone fence. Planes went.
The runway lights were bits of mercury.
We'd take off with him, silver, leave.

Soon I felt the blue rows
of light whip through me—
the airfield adrift, the portholes
tailing off till none of us was there.

    2   Arrival Gate

Black smudges on the sky
send out weak gusts.
My ears are plugged. I'm home.

We go back arm in arm.
He thinks he's a borough or a gaze.
"Who do I belong to?" his face says.

We both left here and came back;
I left again. Now he's stunned,
eternal, white-haired, not at all smug,

and he's small. How is it
he's so small? He tugs my sleeve
as we start toward the baggage check.

He says, "Your eyes are expressionless.
Why, in heaven we settle no scores.
There are no ceilings. Everything's flexible.

Not one soul knows algebra.
There are no scenes, none at all."
How scenic he still is, I think.

But he's different. Who'd have thought
he'd end up wistful, blundering,
tender, embarrassed, and brave?

I never lost him; I ran away.
I reconnoitered childhood,
lived like the ambassador

of a small but strategically-placed
foreign country who'd decided
to be very diplomatic.

He couldn't catch me at sums,
couldn't find me at school.
I was in the needle's eye.

Now we start toward the escalator;
neither one of us sets the pace.
We stare through glass walls, a bit aghast

at the city's bridges—
smokeless, geometric,
those glittering throats.

From a distance, the city's deathless.
Its million windows
stack fire. "How did this tinder

get started?" he asks.
"Who are these people?
How is it I'm so small?

Are you happy? Are you hungry?
What happened to us?
Are we home now?"

IV

In memory of my father,
A. Andrew Widerkehr

Snapshot

When the sea holds its breath as the next wave gathers,
I wonder if the soul persists
into the next world.

When the snow flies over the down-turned faces of children
hurrying home, does the snow erase
only what's unnecessary?

I think of you in that snapshot, bare-chested, holding an infant
in the crook of your arm. It's me you're holding,
as if no one else existed.

Doors

> *the sills of the exquisite, flexible doors...*
> Walt Whitman

Since you left us, all doorways are porous.
Tell me, in the next life, has the sea made peace
    with the incessant shore?

When you lay, unbreathing, chin to the ceiling,
    gaunt and hawk-like,
I thought, *How bleak, how beautiful your face in death!*

Today I stood in synagogue and said *Kaddish*,
as you said it for Grandpa for one year—
    Yisgadal Veyiskadash Sh'may Rabbo...

Magnified and Sanctified
May His Great Name Be
In the World He Created,
As He Wills...

As soon as you were reduced to ashes,
the doors opened, and the sea, which we thought had meant peace,
    began beating against the headstone of the shore.

Pishke

Fire eats twigs, prayer books, flesh, bone.
Perhaps, it eats memories, too.

What about your *pishke?*
That box your parents kept in their kitchen
to put pennies in for the poor.

"We give charity. We don't take charity," Baba said.

In a photo from 1938,
Murray, Irving, Sam, Clara, Larry, and you all stand,
the men wearing suits, except for Larry, a teenager.
He's wearing knickers, he's the only one smiling.
Grandpa sits slewed to one side, his Slavic face jaunty
yet almost bored. Baba sits up straight, stern-faced,
the folds of her black, high-necked dress draping down
to her sturdy black shoes.

It's a formal picture, the barest hint of a smile on Irving's face.
You're twenty-four, assistant manager at Coleman and Company,
sporting a thin mustache so you'd look older, you said.
Your posture rigid, dark eyes intense.
You told me someone once wrote you a letter of recommendation:
"His habits are correct." You were proud of that.

Your income tax for that year lists Baba as a dependant,
the reason, "Unable to support herself."
And Grandpa was working part-time in his mannequin store.

When you went to work at sixteen, the rent got paid.
Before that, Baba sometimes pawned her gold chain, and sometimes
the furniture was put out on the street,
though her credit was still good at the grocery store.

"She never amounted to anything," you said,
"but she was a somebody."

I put these words in no *pishke*,
as I gaze at your proud face in this fading picture
whose occasion—was it Clara's wedding?—
I never thought to ask you.

"Come Here," Said the Burning Angel, and You Said, "Here I Am"

A train goes down its track, rounds a curve—
there, at the end, did you see the engine
that had been hauling you for ninety-one years?

Perhaps, it rose up like a white mountain of truth and minutiae.

You used to say white lies
are lies told for someone else's benefit,
like your not telling Baba you took the plane, and not the train,
to Detroit on business each month.

"Whose benefit was that for?" Linda asks.

I think of the time you smiled with affection and said to your brothers,
"She's still *nudzhing me*," when she was nearly ninety.

Meaning Baba, who never *nudzhed Grandpa* or told him what to do.
She just explained what would happen
if he did this, what would happen if he did that.

"So she was never wrong!" you said, shaking your head,
laughing with rueful wonder.

On our mantle, I have her brass candlesticks you left me.

They crossed the Atlantic from Brezzan, in Austria-Hungary,
to Brooklyn, went to Detroit, back to New York,
and sped across the country with you to Oregon.

I have your black wool jacket, your journals, your chess set,
but I'm losing you.

Or I must release you
in anecdotes and dust, old tax returns,
signed in a neat script with your blue fountain pen.

Tell me, since God warned Moses, "You can't see my face and live,"
does that imply we see God in the next life?
Will I see you?

Tell me a shining white lie.

My Father in His Office

This smiling man in a bow tie and white shirt, how many columns
        of figures has he added?

The metal file cabinets behind him, his files not in manila envelopes,
        but in mailing envelopes from companies' annual reports.
Way back then you were recycling, a penny saved,
        better in your pocket than in someone else's.

Right up to the end, you had Mom buy those Safeway boxes
        of powdered milk, and each day
she mixed in the water to make skim milk.
"My wife can afford whole milk," you said. "I can't."

The man in this photo has come through the war and the Depression
        when people were scared, but you said, "I was never scared."

In one of the books on your shelf, *Ride a Tiger,* the hero wonders
        if he'd be seen as less of a man, less a *shtarker,*
if he showed he was afraid. You underlined the passage, using a ruler,
        a life-long student.

When my lit teacher in college asked us to tell about our fathers,
        I said, "My Dad's an accountant,"
but the prof thought I said "coward" and chewed me out.

You weren't a coward, and not about dying.
On the day of your surgery, you said,
        "It's in the lap of the gods. If I've got to go,
I've got to go. It's no tragedy. I've had a good run."

Your definition of a friend, someone who'll do things for you
        after you're gone.

How broadly you smile out of this snapshot.
I wish I'd asked you its occasion and who took the picture.

"I am the atonement for my father's rest,"
a phrase in the prayer book.

Though I told you I loved you at the end,
I can't seem to cancel the old accounts or close the book—

can't divide zero into you and not get infinity.

February

The steam shovel bites into yellowish-brown earth.
Cold sunshine, and some of the blossoms have already opened.

Boxcars on a siding, heavy with cargo, and clouds pile up
        on the horizon.

I think of that picture of you, smiling, in your office.
Grandpa had promised you a watch if you worked in his store
        the summer you were thirteen.
At the end of the summer, he couldn't afford to buy the watch.

"A promise is a *promise*," you said. "And a promise to a child...."

You always enjoyed your work.
"If you don't like your job, you should quit," you said.
"If the *shtupping* you're giving isn't worth
        the *shtupping* you're getting...."

I look at my notes of what doctors and nurses told me
        those last two months of your life—
times you were agitated, dehydrated, and one time you thought
        there'd been some big *charade* the night before.
"Were you in on it?" you asked me. "They had me walking
        miles and miles up and down the halls."
And one time, you saw ghosts, and the next day,
        I said you'd been confused.

"I was more than confused. I was *delusional*."

The steam shovel bites into the raw earth.
Some blossoms that opened have closed up again.

Mountain

It's rained almost forty nights since the night you died.
Having no ark, I set out to climb you, the only mountain I know,
      but haven't gotten past this pile of ledgers, journals,
and tax returns going back to the 1930's.

I can't even seem to reach your ankles, your knees.

When I sang to you in Green Valley, as you sat in your wheelchair,
      down the hall from your demented roommate—
grim-faced, you listened to my concert, you called it.

> *Summertime and the livin' is easy,*
> *Fish are jumpin' and the cotton's high.*
> *Oh, your daddy's rich, and your mama's good-lookin',*
> *So hush, little baby, don't you cry.*

Hearing's the last of our senses to go, I'm told.

Now we've come to the sweet by-and-by where the hazy promises
      of yesterday present their bills to be paid.
Buds open in February, this mild winter, yet snow on the foothills
      tastes like regret.

I fill up pages as if I were climbing toward you, and maybe I am.

The pine tree Linda planted leans away from the larger alder tree
      beside it.
What I leaned away from always is missing.

All the times my train pulled away from the station,
      it was as if I were a planet
that had once more escaped the pull of some larger planet.

I still felt your hand gripping mine as you thanked me
        for coming down.

"Tell Linda I'm not such a son-of-a-bitch," you said.

I cried when I got the news,
and she said, "You loved him very much, and he knew it."

Tonight, this gibbous moon, first one in weeks, more faceless
        than a man in a Plexiglas helmet, riding away—

it seems futile to mention the moon. It isn't you.
How slowly it climbs the sky.

Do you lie face up, under the white cliffs of heaven,
the slopes of your shoulders touching the sky?

The snows on your lips can't melt.

Pony

Perhaps, when you were a boy, you had those blinding,
        diamond-blue skies
the day after a big snow, as I did.

From the time you were five years old,
        you were a grown-up, you told me.
They wanted you to start school when you were five,
        but you said, "I'll go when I'm six."

And you did.

"I knew I'd be going to school *a long time*," you said.

It's as if we're sitting in a darkened living room,
        and a projectionist's setting up one of those portable screens,
so we can see these faded memories,
        flickering on his screen.

In one snapshot, you're up on a spotted pony,
        maybe six-years-old.
Soup-bowl haircut, stern-faced, in front of your stoop
        right there on Rivington Street.

A Jewish pony?
You, on a pony of all things!

What With the Snow

What with the snow, its heavy flakes falling on the swings
        in the park where the dying old man sits singing, "Life is Brief,"
a scene in Kurosawa's *Ikiru* Linda and I watched last night—

I think of you, not loving life at the end, but raging
        at your roommate at Green Valley,
that thin, smiling guy with Alzheimer's who kept stealing your walker.

"Make him give that back," you demanded. "It has *my* name on it!"

And when he called the black aide *boy*, you yelled,
        "Who's he calling *boy*? Didn't Lincoln free the slaves in 1865?"

You had the nurse position your bed at the exact midpoint of the room,
        right under the clock, fifty-fifty, even-steven.

I told you your roommate's confused.

"He's more than confused," you said. "It's his *personality*."

What can you tell me about streets, stars, anger?
Perhaps, when you broke your hip, you knew the end was near.

What can you say about cities, about the sloping shoulders of old men
        playing chess in the park?
What about the boxcar in the middle of an unfinished bridge in Israel,
        a memorial to the Holocaust?

You told me, "Gandhi said the Jews should've committed
        mass suicide to show the world what was happening.
We didn't know anything, but Roosevelt and Churchill did."

What can you say about snow, a taste of snow, as it melted?

What about the almost-full moon, low in the sky, as we raced
        down the freeway to see you?

What about oatmeal, pea soup, and pureed meatloaf
you made yourself eat at the end?

It wasn't snowing when your soul departed from your body.
You weren't singing in that park with its empty swings.

The Will

*White, black, white—those wings
flashed, then disappeared....*

You left me five per cent, a slap in the face.

As you lay in your hospital bed, two weeks after surgery,
I held your hand. "I feel you prefer
him to me," I said.
                "I don't prefer him.
I prefer his business sense. I prefer that you're *you*.
I didn't manufacture an accountant, but someone
who can stand on his own feet."

And so that was my blessing, my portion.

Also the flock of dunlins I saw
the day you went back into the hospital—
how they kept circling over that low island
in Padilla Bay,
         *flashing in and out
of this life and some second life....*

At dinner, Linda said, "It isn't Jeffrey
who takes the train to see him each month,
who calls him each week."

That evening, I called—
your vitals unstable, fingernails blue. The nurse
had called 911, but you told her, "Your equipment's faulty,"
and refused to go to the hospital. "They treat me
like a bag of potatoes!"

I told you to go, and you went,
not because I asked you to, but because the nurse
and I agreed and you respected her opinion.

One of the few times I can remember
your doing what I suggested.

I've read that dunlins, in slow motion,
move in a wave. How that whole flock kept flashing
in loops and skeins, figure eights—then for one second
an hourglass, a double helix—all those wings,
flickering and vying.

A hint of what the next world is like?
A world made of light, where (is it true?)
God keeps faith with those who sleep in the dust.

Three Wishes

My train doesn't bring me closer. The clouds glide farther away.
        Did I think you'd keep cheating death forever?

It seems you're both true and untrue now, or your proof
        is elusive, like the one for prime numbers.

What about the number five, the per cent you left me,
        or our racing down the freeway to see you?

Take walks, dinners, phone calls, how at last I held your hand,
        multiply them, square the product, add one. Is it you?

You said fairy tales teach us how having three wishes, for instance,
        means there are limits, even when dealing with magic,

and having one wish at a time means we can have what we want,
        but only at the price of not having everything else.

At the end, when the burning wings came closer, what did you
        wish for? Did you pause at the top of the stairs?

Boxer Shorts

I picture you in faded, blue cotton boxer shorts, back in the fifties.
You're wearing those shorts and your thin, sleeveless undershirt,
        the kind that looks like it has straps.

It's after midnight, summer, hot as hell, and you've gotten up from bed
        to hunt down a mosquito
in our apartment in Forest Hills, New York, so you can sleep.

Rolled-up newspaper in one hand, you stand on a chair,
lips pursed with grim determination, the same grit and *chutzpah*
        that got you through nine years of night school at City College
as you worked days at Coleman and Company, back in the Depression.

And now you hunt the fierce Forest Hills mosquito,
its low whine an affront to all you've worked for, its bite an insult
        to be deeply resented.

When, after circling and circling, it alights on the wall,
you whack and whack it.

How methodical your cold, righteous anger,
as when you turned Mom over your knee once and spanked her
after she threw her coffee cup at you.

Can you sleep now, can you breathe easy?
Can you rest in peace?

Moses Standing on His Head

A taste of metal in my mouth, the five per cent you left me,
        two paintings, Baba's candlesticks,
your hands gripping mine.

The smell of mothballs in your closet, as I take down
        your long, black wool overcoat,
like a rabbi's coat.

Two pennies on your eyelids, a tarnished, black spoon.

Dunlins flashing in and out of the light, disappearing,
        can't speak for you.

"Once, it can happen," you said. "Twice, you're stupid. Three times,
        you have to be an idiot."

Abraham Andrew "Andy," born in Brooklyn, New York—
        because I loved you, in spite of everything,
I hold out my hands.

Moishe kapoyr, Moses standing on his head,
though Moses was rebuked for letting on that he and not God
        drew water from the rock.

Perhaps, you too have been rebuked,
permitted to see, but not enter, the promised land.

Not yet done with the bland oatmeal of regret,
        not yet feasting on manna.

How you left twelve blue roses on Mom's table once.

I keep your shoe trees in my closet and wear two watches,
        as you did.

If we meet in the next world, I'll put on your long, black coat.
Perhaps, we'll stroll beneath *Sheol's* bare, black trees.

Or it'll be summer, and you'll be wearing blue cotton boxer shorts,
        standing on a chair at midnight, fist upraised,
drawing water from the bitter rock.

Remember Me

Half-mad Hamlet, how he tried to be true
to his father's ghost, his *Remember me!*

And though revenge went against his nature,
Hamlet tried to whip himself to it.

How your anger was a fire you kept nursing
and giving dress rehearsals,

telling Mom she'd done nothing right for sixty years,
or: "If it's right, it's a mistake."

In that book on your shelf, *Ride a Tiger,* you underlined the part
about the hero's anger, how it gave him clarity.

As for me, when I work in the hospital,
perhaps it's so that, like you, I can do something useful.

Is the sky useful? In my twenties, when I carried my briefcase
on the subway in New York,

as you once did, I wondered: Was I the proof
of your life's theorem?

Grandpa and Baba, did they come all this way from Brezzan
so I might smudge some words on a page?

Brezzan, near Lvov, now in the Ukraine, once in Poland,
once in Lithuania, and once in Austria-Hungary,

where armies fought *to gain a little patch of ground*
that hath in it no profit but a name.

How can I be true to you, when fire took you
and finally consumed you?

Today, the sun's spread out in the sky, a gray-white ghost.
I say my prayer for you.

Making Your Bed

Huge trees bend down under the weight
    of what's happened.

I cling to your words, as at the end
    you clung to my hands.

A few weeks before your fall,
you asked me to help make your bed.

Like everything else, it had to be done just so.
"Do it right the first time," you always said.

Ninety-one-years old, you gamely supervised.
"No, not like that."

First, the mattress cover had to be tucked under the mattress.
Each sheet and blanket tucked in one at a time,
    first at the bottom, then on one side,
leaving four inches of blanket and sheet
    draped over the other side of the bed.

I thought of how you used to brush your hair
one hundred strokes, morning and night.

No trial and error for you,
No helter-skelter mishmash of clouds and wind,
leaving a mess for someone else.

"Actions speak louder than words," you said.

What bed do you lie down in?
Is it all right now?
Can you rest?

Ledger

My train hauls itself from the station
into the dark fir trees.

Arched iron bridges can't carry me to you.

What about your double entry ledger,
in which you recorded the stocks you transferred to us,
year by year?

It's still on your desk.

Last year, you bought a "put" on the euro,
to have a little fun, you said.

I've stopped saying *Kaddish* for you every day,
just once a month now at the synagogue.

I write this, my single entry, in your memory.
The broad, brown river glides away.

Black Clarinet

The clarinet, a comedian, knows that snow is an oboe,
regret's a black flute.

When you drove me past the train station in Ann Arbor
       forty years ago,
the merchants had draped blue and gold banners
over the streets, "Welcome Students!"

You said what they should've said was "Welcome Suckers."

What about your coming into the spare bedroom
when I visited last winter? You in your white long underwear.
Mom had turned up the thermostat to eighty degrees.

"Can't you *do* something about it?
Make her turn it down!"

I told you I couldn't.

"If you can't, you can't."

Who'll guard your rest now, your bed of black snapdragons?

Who'll carry your hat with the plastic rain cover
into the rain?

Who'll remember your story of chocolate,
how when you were thirteen it melted,
and you had to eat the profits.

What about anger with its red trumpets,
its yellow kettles and snares?

Can you hear me?
Or is your journey like looking out the rear window of a train speeding away from a station where no one gets off or on?

Who'll hold your hand? Who'll sing to you?
Who'll say when?

Snow

Take snow's architecture, breath. Take the structure of water,
        tetrahedrons or tiny rings and chains,
physicists can't agree.

Take the time you said I was callow,
        you were callous.

Or the time I told you I planned to major in English
and you spit out your inimitable word, *Puh!*

Take how, last year, you bought copies of my novel
        and gave them to your friends.

Take snow, the way it once melted.

No Clouds, No Wind

No huge, black Gearbulk freighters rising up from the horizon
        like apparitions,
no grocery receipts to add up, no number to give for regret,
        no one to write into or out of your will,
no extra containers of talcum powder or dental floss to clear out
        of your room,
no one to listen to the wind's diatribes, the rain's mistakes,
no one to tell how the father in *The 10,000* really loved his son,
        though his son didn't think so.

There's no stopping the obsessive rain rattling the thick windows,
        the tugboats hauling their cargo of days.

No one to tell how you sometimes went to strangers' weddings
        in the Depression, to get a free meal.
How strange, there seems to be more to say,
        now that you're gone.

The rain ticking against the windows reminds me how you showed me
        Zuckertort's beautiful queen and rook sacrifice ending in mate.
On my shelf, a book of yours I haven't yet read,
        The Art of Sacrifice in Chess.

What I've won is what you gave freely, yourself—
        difficult, surprising, intrusive, intelligent, childish, child-like,
brutal, charming, argumentative.

My cousin Judy says whenever you called her,
        it was like the Hebrew National Hotdogs commercial,
clouds and that voice, a call from a higher authority.

How mean you were to Mom at the end, telling her she raised us kids
        all wrong, not letting her touch you.

Are you *kibbitzing* the ferry man as he makes this crossing,
      showing him how he could run his business more efficiently,
asking the man upstairs how he got into his line of work?

Are you telling him, as you planned to, that you did your best?

La Jolla

I don't weep when I look at this picture.
It's 1943, you're wearing a tan uniform,
just starting to break into a smile. The two of you,
standing on a beach in California, near La Jolla,
where you were stationed for a while, chief warrant officer,
during the war.
                        She's smiling, she's so young!
You're both so young, it's as if you're strangers
to me almost, though I can see the faint resemblance
to the Mom and Dad I'll come to know.

Both of you dark-haired and trim, posture straight—
you seem ready for anything, though you can't know yet
how troubled your marriage will be, or how Helen's mental illness
and Chloe's lie waiting.

I think of Delmore Schwartz who wanted to warn
his parents not to have children,
though I don't want to tell you that, even though
Mom tells me she's glad
Linda and I don't have children so that gene
isn't passed on.

As you stand on that sandy beach,
small white cabins behind you,
as you smile into the distance of that war
your generation will win—
                            I want to tell you
how happy I am to have this picture.
What I want you to tell me—
that you won't leave.

A Big Fir Tree, Uprooted

                    1

At its base, a gibberish of twisted roots, dangling,
a wall of dark earth.
High above it, an eagle slowly, heavily, beating its wings.

How garbled your speech got toward the end—
the devil and the deep blue sea, Scylla and Charybdis,
no time to get a message to Garcia.

Then, quite clearly: "There's nothing they can do for me."

The last night we talked on the phone, lots of static.
Your voice grim and grating, indignant.
"They gave me the wrong tray for breakfast. I didn't eat it.
But I keep on punching."

How you hung on, down to 120 pounds.
So many things gone wrong—heart, lungs, broken hip,
that bedsore on your heel they operated on.

I keep telling people things you said,
how you liked to quote your friend Gottschaulk
at Coleman and Company,
an intelligent man without an education,
who said, "You can loin a lot if you obsoive tings."

This morning, on the radio, a haiku by Kerouac:

> *Dusk—*
> *the blizzard hides*
> *even the night.*

2

Is it night where you are? Is it cold?
Are you asking Socrates what he thinks and saying, "Not just that"?

Or are you asking your namesake, Abraham,
what he thinks of that crazy sacrifice God demanded?

Baba called you Abe. You were Andy to everyone else.
Your signature, A. Andrew Widerkehr, a neat script.

The nurse who straightened your sheets, from the bottom,
        as you instructed,
did her best, and when you said, "They're not straight,"
she replied, "They're as straight as they're going to get, Andy."

This tree with its root-ball of dark marl—
is that what having a heart attack is like? A last judgment?

It's three months since you left us.

How can it be March, buds opening?
How can this eagle be bearing a twig back to its empty nest?

Shadow Boxing

And now these white blossoms floating, like the final chord
       of Sibelius's seventh symphony,
as if he knew it would be his last.

Forty years ago, you dreamt you were falling
       to earth from black space,
saying, "Eternity, here I come!"

In that snapshot of you in your twenties,
       you stand on a dirt road, wearing a bathing suit,
hands on hips, trim and fit as a welterweight
       daring anyone to challenge him.

Once, you stood up to a bully
       who'd been picking on Larry.
"I kept aiming for the same spot. Take whatever punishment
       you have to, but keep hitting him in the eye."

Grandpa asked, "How could you be so stupid,
       to get in a fight?"
"I know," you said, "but sometimes you can't avoid it."

You were in your eighties when you told me this story,
       still swimming or walking each day.
As you bobbed and threw mock punches,
       I thought of how you'd spar with me when I was a kid,
putting one hand on top of my head,
       holding me away.

Has the next life worked out as you planned?
Is it the doughnut or the hole in the doughnut, as you used to say?

Whatever it is, it can't be spring, white blossoms floating.

Crossing the Water

Will I carry a sad angel's Menorah toward you
into the next world?

Will you see the lights I light for you?
Will we play chess or argue politics?

Will we walk on the Lower East Side down Rivington
toward Broome Street?

Will we run together over the Brooklyn Bridge
as you did when you were young?

Will we wait on the ferry or disembark
at the final destination?

Different from streets or grief,
your face stays with me, the one poem I write.

Six Degrees of Freedom

The far-off, sandy spit in shadow, the eroding yellow bluffs
    in sunlight,
this ferry boat pitching and rolling in the big swells—

I've heard how there are six degrees of freedom—
yaw, pitch, roll, and translation of motion,
    the four I remember.

I know about the pitch of memory, the yaw of regret,
and there's this steady rolling passage wherein I translate you.

Perhaps, you might like my writing about you—you said
    you liked my putting you in my novel.

What this crossing is about, after all, is gratitude—
I felt you somewhere nodding in approval
when I took the two paintings you left me.

I've yet to learn all six degrees of freedom.
For now there's just this pitching and rolling, the enormous yaw
    at the end of your crossing.

Horses Grazing

Perhaps, it isn't just hunger
that bends their graceful necks
to the grass.

I carry my grief into bright air
on a day I spent figuring my taxes.
My *taxes!*

A red-tailed hawk glides by, high above.

I can't go with you into the tunnels
beneath hunger and dread.

In whatever alphabet or garden you find yourself,
what facts are you facing?
What numeral is true?

You who are now part of what no one can deny or refute—
at the end of snowfall and dust,
at the end of sunlight,
at the end of the rain on the rubble
of the fatherless cities....

At the end of your journey, when you bowed down,
did you remember how sweet life was,
how brief?

Blue As Twilight

Are you moving or still?
Are you wind, ash, old photos, a white glimmer in a doorway,
        a guest that can't leave?

Or are you some light-absorbing color
          grief can't reach?

Here, April goes on with its business,
fleshing out some unseen thought, not saying whose.

And if by keeping silent, I might learn the language
        you speak now, I'd shut my trap.

Is it snowing where you are, and you chase white butterflies,
          fragile blossoms, not saying which is which?

About the Author

Richard Widerkehr won two Hopwood Awards for poetry at the University of Michigan, where he earned his B.A. in English. He received his M.A. from Columbia University, which he attended on a Woodrow Wilson Fellowship. He won first prize for a short story at the Pacific Northwest Writers Conference and three awards in *The Bridge's* annual poetry contests.

Pudding House Publications published his chapbook of poems, *Mountain,* and Radiolarian Press published his chapbook, *Disappearances*. Tarragon Books published his novel about a geologist, *Sedimental Journey*. His poems and stories have appeared in *Chariton Review, Pontoon, Passages North, Northwest Poets and Artists Calendar, Crab Creek Review, Writers' Forum,* and *Salt River Review*.

Widerkehr lives in Washington State, where he has been a teacher in the Upward Bound program, a case manager at a mental health clinic, and a counselor on the mental health unit of a hospital.

www.ingramcontent.com/pod-product-compliance
Lightning Source LLC
Chambersburg PA
CBHW052108070526
44584CB00017B/2396